Choice Is Your SuperPower!®

7 Surprisingly Simple Steps to Break Through Your Boundaries, Skyrocket Your Self-Confidence, and Unleash Your Inner Genius - Starting Today!

Deb Dredden

DEB DREDDEN
TRANSFORMATIONAL COACHING

Choice Is Your SuperPower!® *7 Surprisingly Simple Steps to Break Through Your Boundaries, Skyrocket Your Self-Confidence, and Unleash Your Inner Genius- Starting Today!* by Deb Dredden

Published by Deb Dredden Transformational Coaching, LLC

Salt Lake City, Utah

Debdredden.com

Copyright © 2022 Deb Dredden
9798840309179

First Edition

Other Works by Deb Dredden

10 Proven Power Principles for a Successful and Rewarding Life

The Power of Mindset to Change Your Life!

Shatter Your Negative Self-Image and Skyrocket Your Self-Confidence!

5 Steps to Transform Your Pain into a Lifetime of Gain

Being Mindful in the Midst of Chaos

Escape Your Groundhog Day and Create the Life You Love

Gratitude Journal

Crush Your Limiting Beliefs

The 5-Step Blueprint to Find Your Passion and Begin Living Your Life with Purpose!

Contents

Other Works by Deb Dredden 3

Testimonials 7

Foreward 12

Who Should Read This Book 16

Here's My Promise to You 19

Who am I, and Why did I Write this Book? 22

Your Honest Assessment 25

Start With Your Owner's Manual 36

Your Operating System 39

Step #1: Amp Your Awareness 47

Step #2: Understand Which Circle You're In 51

Step #3: Use Your Superpower! 55

Step #4: Source For Solutions 63

Step #5: Visualize Your Outcome 68

Step #6: Apply Action To Get Traction! 75

Step #7: Hold Yourself Accountable To You! 80

Success Stories 89

Next Steps 97

Frequently Asked Questions 102

Acknowledgments 106

About The Author 108

Appendix/Resources 110

Testimonials

"An uncommonly powerful Coach, Deb Dredden consistently demonstrates a high level of awareness combined with a gift for asking simple yet deeply thought-provoking questions and a laser-focus on results. Deb has significantly contributed to my growth and the growth of my business. If you are seriously seeking positive, sustainable change, I strongly recommend you engage Deb Dredden and lean into the process!"
~ Kathy Young, CEO/Founder, Carlson/Young, Inc

"Our firm engaged Deb on several occasions to provide professional Coaching for employees. The results were positive - very positive - and furthered the careers of employees while increasing the firm's ability to execute profitably. I strongly endorse Deb in terms of her ability to address organizational blind spots, develop struggling team members, and help leaders develop to their potential. Work every cent of the INVESTMENT in people, time, and success of the business!"
~ Dr. Jeffrey Ahrstrom, CEO at Ingersoll Machine Tools

"Deb is a great listener and communicator. She excels at asking questions to get you to insights that drive self-awareness. She has the ability to Coach and develop leaders to their full potential. Deb

truly brings out the best in everyone she comes into contact with. Her positive energy is contagious, and her approach is respected by all. She lives every day with a relentless pursuit to be the best at whatever she is doing which ignites others and delivers results. I would give my highest recommendation to anyone considering transformational Coaching- you will most definitely benefit from your experience with Deb!" ~ Dana Kleifges, VP Salon and Support Operations for Hair Cuttery

"Role model. Leader. Coach. Champion maker. Friend. Since she founded DDTC, I have had the honor of working with her to develop my leader within. She Coached me through some rough waters and helped me identify the tools that enabled me to row myself to the calmer seas and stay there, and to be a better leader for my team. She is an amazing Coach and person that truly cares about people and helping them to become their very best. If you are looking to develop yourself or leaders within your team/company, there is none better than Deb!" ~ Diana Paine, Global Travel Manager for Halliburton

"Deb Dredden is the epitome of a Transformational Life Coach from which any organization would benefit. She is a servant leader and Coach that exudes characteristics that all leaders should have. She has an effortless talent for transformational Coaching and developing others in ways others could not imagine." ~Tamara Dancy, SHRM-CP, PHR

"Deb's ability to Coach and encourage her team so eloquently is remarkable. She is one of the most motivational and encouraging humans I have ever worked for." ~ Julia Gibas. Strategic Operations Manager and Director of Communication, Stanton Chase

"Deb Dredden is one of the most influential people in my career. She has a unique ability to foster self-awareness; she leads this through effective Coaching to create a culture of successful independent leaders. She provides an unparalleled development rich culture; you walk away from each conversation with Deb not only learning more, but most importantly learning more about yourself." ~ Bridgette Murphy, Flagship General Manager, American Eagle Outfitters

"Deb is a fantastic Coach and is able to maximize each employee's talents. Deb was a key in identifying my strengths and weaknesses and helped develop my career."
~ Chad Feather, Vice President Financial Solutions, First Commonwealth Bank

"Deb has been my mentor and life Coach for over 20 years. Her advice and training have driven me to achieve my goals in work and personal life. I would give my highest recommendation to anyone who is really interested in achieving their full potential." ~ Jana Whitmore, Banker at Rocket Mortgage

"Deb carries herself with complete professionalism and operates with the highest level of integrity. She manages as a servant leader and inspires leaders to be their best and execute responsibilities while maintaining the same high standards she models herself. I found her to be the most influential role model of all of the multi-unit managers I have worked with in my 10 years in retail, and 8 years in management." ~ Rod Shiva, Director of Customer Delight at ListReports

""Deb is a smart, compassionate, trustworthy, and encouraging individual who has an incredible ability to help others sort through difficult or challenging circumstances. She is a great listener who is patient and insightful. She is extremely personable and has the ability to connect with people quickly. Deb excels at helping people gain clarity, set goals and create next steps all with a great level of encouragement and support along the way. I have known Deb for over 20 years, and I can tell you Deb has always loved and excelled in Coaching and helping others achieve and this passion is evident in all she does. Hire Deb! You will not be disappointed."
~ Michelle Martin, Board Member, Leadership Advisor, Senior Retail Executive

This book is dedicated to my superhero husband,
Patrick, because YOU are my
BEST choice.

Foreword

C ontrary to popular belief, luck, circumstance, academic prowess, being born into the "right" family, or even experience is not what determines success in life. There are many, if not more examples of where such factors have proved to be more of a hindrance than an advantage.

We're wired, raised, programmed, and conditioned to look for reasons—or more often than not, *excuses*—for why we come up short, struggle, fail…and why other people seem to get the breaks we long for.

Every time we look in the wrong place for the solutions to our most pressing needs, wants, and challenges, it's not because we're dumb, stupid or incompetent, but because we know no better.

The answer, the way forward, the breakthrough is *always* within—we're just not conscious of it.

Don't downplay what holding this short, yet powerful, book in your hand demonstrates: It makes you atypical and puts you a very small percentage of our species.

Whatever brought you here, you know there's more to life and more to you than is currently showing up in your results—and you're curious enough to explore beyond the grossly limited perspective of "conventional wisdom."

You have my word. If you're willing to make that a philosophy for life, you'll be rewarded in ways you can't even imagine.

What you'll discover within these pages will—*if you allow it*—radically improve your life—as long as you're willing to embrace the ideas, concepts and principles, and, most importantly, to put them to work.

The tools of any craftsman can't do the job at hand alone, and any method of personal transformation can't do its work unless you bring you to the table.

The power is within you—this book is the catalyst by which you start to unlock it. Only then can it show up in your results.

Do not underestimate what you have in your hands. I'm not a man known for making claims of this magnitude lightly when it comes to recommending works of this nature. All too often those claims are hyped-up, misleading hyperbole… which leads me to the most important point of all:

Who you learn from matters more than what you learn. In a world where everyone claims to be a "Coach" these days – and so very few making the claim are - you have to be very careful about the integrity and trustworthiness of the individual making the claim.

I can make this assertion simply because Coaching is my business. At the time of writing, I'm in my third decade in the industry and I've brought industry-leading Coaching training and mentoring to in excess of 40,000 Coaches from over 170 countries. My Clients have included some of the biggest names in the self-improvement industry, including the late Bob Proctor and John C. Maxwell.

All this to say, I know a false "Coach" from a real one, and a good Coach from an exceptional one.

In Deb Dredden, you have more than an "exceptional" Coach – you have a truly masterful one.

Here's why you can take my word for it. I've worked closely with Deb for many years. She is one of those 40,000 Coaches I referenced – the only difference is she is one of the top 0.1% in terms of ability.

I not only trained Deb to be a Coach when she first came into the profession, I also personally hand-picked her as a Founding Member of my *Conscious Coaching Academy™* - a privilege only extended to a small group of Coaches who met the most stringent of qualifying criteria.

Make no mistake, you are in the best of hands. Deb Dredden is not only a world-class Coach, she's a phenomenal human being who walks her talk as a leading example of what she asks of her Clients.

The profoundly powerful message she has to share with you is beautifully distilled into seven, simple, practical and easy-to-apply steps, helping you remove the shackles which have denied you up to this point, so you can start to live the life you've long aspired to.

Consider this book your blueprint to the kind of life you'd love to have. And best of all, it's timeless in its application: one of those rare books which you can return to time and time again and it'll never fail to take you to the next level.

Oh, and one final point: if you're fortunate enough to have the opportunity of the privilege of working with Deb Dredden as a Client, don't hesitate: she will bring to you everything you need to become everything you've dreamt of and more.

You'll never make a greater investment, because you're the greatest asset you'll ever… you just don't know it.

Yet.

Enjoy this process of becoming so much more!

Christian Simpson

Who Should Read This Book

Do you feel frustrated and at your wit's end? You don't know where else to go to break free from the pain in your life?

Are you someone who constantly compares yourself, your job, your life to everyone else's and usually decides yours is lacking?

Does a negative body image create feelings of constant disappointment, isolation, or despair because you believe no one can love you just the way you are?

Does your self-doubt keep you stuck at home, perhaps on the couch watching Netflix instead of meeting up with friends or trying to find your soulmate?

Or perhaps you're stuck in a rut at work—you want to advance but feel overlooked and undervalued?

Do you suffer from absolute terror at the idea of having to speak up during a conference call or meeting, much less having to give a speech in front of a group?

Do other people's opinions of you cripple your desire to break out of the numbing routine of your comfort zone?

Are you afraid to take risks because you might fail, make a mistake, or be rejected?

Do you long to repair your rapidly shredding relationships with your spouse, partner, kids, parents, or best friend?

Or maybe you're just sick and tired of not having the time, money, and freedom to live your life the way you've always dreamed.

Do you wish you could get back in the driver's seat and take control of your life? Or perhaps you've never felt like you ever HAD control in the first place.

You might be someone who is looking for additional insight and tools to continue on your path of personal growth and professional success.

Do any of these scenarios describe you?
If you've answered yes, then I want to assure you, this book is meant for YOU!

On the other hand, if you're:

Someone who has no empathy or patience for other people and the problems they're going through—"Why don't they just fix it and move on?" After all, you did, why can't they?

Certain that you are heads and shoulders above everyone else at work—why can't anyone see that?

Someone who is convinced that the problems in your relationships are almost always the fault of the other person.

Always waiting for someone else to apologize because you didn't make the mistake or start the fight.

A person who has little sympathy for someone who made an obvious mistake and should have known better.

Someone who delights in preying on the weaknesses and vulnerabilities of others. After all, it's survival of the fittest.

Someone who has no respect or tolerance for someone else's point of view, and you make a deliberate effort to let them know how many ways they are wrong. It's because of the 'other guy' that the world is going to hell in a handbasket!

A person who believes that your parents, your boss, your politicians, your spouse, your ex-spouse, etc., are to blame for your current situation, condition, or circumstances.

If any of these examples sound like you, then this is probably not your book. Yet you should be one of the first people reading it because your lack of self-awareness is going to continue to create chaos and unhappiness in your life, as well as in the lives of everyone around you. But that's your choice to make. You might want to ask yourself, however, how those choices have been working out for you.

Here's My Promise to You

I understand your skepticism. You've likely already read multiple self-help books, watched YouTube videos, listened to podcasts and Ted Talks, etc. While those are valuable resources, your motivation after engaging with them probably fizzled out without any long-lasting results.

You're tired, frustrated, and may be ready to throw in the towel because, what's the point? Nothing seems to change in your life so you might as well settle for yet another year or decade starring in your very own *Groundhog Day* movie.

Here's what I can promise you.

First, you are not alone. I would venture that many if not most people feel the way you do. Why do I say that? The vast majority of people I talk to and interact with in life share these same stories. Many of the Clients I've worked with have been where you are, too. Notice I said, "been."

Secondly, I can promise you that the principles and ideas that I share in this short book work. I've experienced the transformation in my own life, and in the lives of thousands of people I've Coached over the past three decades. I've read about millions more who have also broken free from the traps in their lives—you can too!

Third, what you will learn in the following pages absolutely can begin transforming your life, starting today. Here's something to remember: What you'll learn sounds ridiculously easy, too easy. Surely all of life's problems won't go away just by understanding that your power to *choose* is the cornerstone of the solution!

And you'd be right. While the principles I share are straightforward and rooted in science and human physiology, the application of those principles is where the hard work begins.

But I can also promise you that, if you apply these principles consistently—and by consistently I mean to the degree that your old, unhealthy habits are broken and replaced by new, energizing, empowering habits that you lean into every day— you *will* experience a radical transformation in your life.

You *will* begin to see relationships mended—or even left behind if they are toxic or no longer serve you.

You *will* see people responding to you differently, as you begin to establish boundaries of behavior that are acceptable or not. People will also respond to you differently because you'll begin showing up differently!

You *will* begin building rock-solid confidence that can enable you to create and execute the plan for your life that—up until now—you didn't believe was possible.

By the time you finish this short book, you *will* know how to get started creating the most exciting year of your life, and the year after that, and the year after that...

How does that sound? What is it worth to you to make a commitment that you'll read this entire book with an open mind—open to the possibility that you have everything within you to formulate the blueprint of a life you create by design, not default? Can you do that? If so, then congratulations, because your life is about to change!

In the words of one of the best actresses of all time in one of her most iconic roles, "Fasten your seatbelts..." and get ready to hop back into the driver's seat of your life!

Who am I, and Why did I Write this Book?

I've been coaching professionally for over 30 years. I've worked with some of the most well-known companies in the states and around the globe. In addition to running my own company, Deb Dredden Transformational Coaching, I'm also an affiliate of the John Maxwell Team, the largest leadership development organization in the world. And I'm proud to be a founding member of the Conscious Coaching Academy, the world's leading Accreditation in the Coaching Industry, created by the world-class Coach himself, Christian Simpson. Throughout this time, I have been fortunate to work with some amazing thought leaders, teachers, Coaches, and mentors, who helped to transform my own life through what you're about to learn.

During all these years of working with bosses, peers, direct reports, and now Clients, I've seen thousands of lives transformed by these same principles, ideas, and actions. Thousands! So, I can say with confidence that these principles are proven. They work!

For me, there has been no more rewarding experience than to be a catalyst for change in someone else's life. As a leading Mindset Expert and Executive Coach running my own business, as well as having been an executive in the retail world for many years, I've been fortunate to be a part of the transformations in the lives of more people than I can count. I consider it a privilege and a gift that keeps on giving.

Yet I want to reach even more people than I can physically impact through Transformational Coaching.

Which is why I wrote this book, and why I want to share these 7 Surprisingly Simple Steps with you, your neighbor, your family, your coworkers—anyone who is willing to read this book and to commit to the ideas within.

As with learning any new skill, it's likely that at some point you will want additional support and structure to help you apply what you're discovering. At certain points in this book I am going to give you the option to book a call with me to explore how the Coaching partnership can create the structure for your sustainable and life-long transformation.

But that's not the main goal of this book. Let me paraphrase that: This is a book meant to equip you to begin solving your own problems, right where you are, with no further investment required than the purchase of this book.

You see, I believe there's no better way to promote my expertise and generate new Clients than to provide real, fail-proof, proven solutions to all the scenarios I spoke of just a few pages back.

Throughout this book I will share tools, exercises, and solutions with you. For easy reference, many are also found in the Appendix of this book.

Once you see what these solutions can do for you, once you experience success firsthand, you may be inclined to recommend this book, my products, and services to other people.

Or maybe after experiencing the solutions, you'd like to stretch your results even further by working with me one-on-one. I don't work with everyone, but I have a few spots available for people who are genuinely serious about wanting to accelerate their transformation and take things to the next level. But again—that is not the purpose of this book.

The purpose of this book is to equip you with tools that will put you in the driver's seat of your own life so that *you* are in control! You set the course as you create a life you love by design, not default!

Your Honest Assessment

S o, let's talk about what might be troubling you for a minute. Here are three scenarios that I've found to be common amongst many of my Clients.

Scenario #1: You're concerned about your current job/boss/ company
You are stuck in a job you used to like, but for so long you have wanted to advance/get promoted so that you can more effectively put your skills and abilities to work for the benefit of others and the organization.

As you look around, there are other people you perceive to be smarter and more talented, and who have an "in" with the boss that you don't have, so they are likely to be promoted ahead of you, keeping you stuck where you are. And you're not willing to go along to get along—you feel that it compromises your integrity.

You try to speak up, add value, and get the respect you know you deserve, but it seems your voice is never heard or appreciated. The boss plays favorites, constantly overlooks you, and you don't even really like the job you're doing anymore. You feel overworked, undervalued, and stagnant. There's GOT to be more, you tell yourself. But this job pays the bills, and after all, it's too late in the game to change careers...so you stay stuck.

Scenario #2: You feel acute loneliness, isolation, and deep feelings of inadequacy

You've been alone for so long—the pandemic has isolated you from socializing with others or from forming new friendships or relationships.

Yet even in your intense desire to be among other people and to be loved, you are plagued by feelings of self-doubt and inadequacy. You constantly compare yourself to others and find yourself deficient in so many areas. The idea of getting out of your comfort zone and risking getting hurt continues to keep you isolated.

At the heart of it, you just don't believe you have what it takes to build lasting relationships because no one could love you just the way you are. You're obsessed with wanting to change aspects of yourself and your life, but have no idea how, so you might as well accept the fact that you're destined to be alone or in bad relationships for the rest of your life. Yet the idea of that scenario is soul-crushing, so you continue to search for a solution somewhere, anywhere, just to make the pain stop.

Scenario #3: You long for the freedom, creativity, and possibility that could come with being your own boss

You've always wanted to be an entrepreneur, set your own course, and have the freedom that brings to your life.

But you're not really sure how to get started, or even how to determine what you're passionate about in order to start your own business.

You might be thinking that even considering going off on your own is highly irresponsible because you have a family to support, kids to put through college, and a budget that takes every dollar you and your spouse generate. You should just be thankful for the job you do have and stop daydreaming about unrealistic aspirations. Suck it up and get on with your life—it's not so bad, after all, others have it much worse than you do. Yet the idea of year after year spent in your current situation feels so empty and pointless. But you put your dreams back on the dusty shelf and tell yourself to get your head out of the clouds, be an adult, and take care of your responsibilities.

Do you recognize yourself in any of these scenarios? If so, you are definitely not alone!

Let me be very candid here. The problem most people have is that they often believe they are victims of circumstances, conditions, biology, or geography, and they allow these beliefs to define them and limit their potential, however subconsciously.

Where many people get stuck:

- They act and react based on habit, and often those habits don't serve them in any healthy way.

Here's a sobering statistic for you—research has shown that up to 95% of what we do on a daily basis is habitual. *Think about that for a minute!* Up to 95% of the time we're not even consciously aware of these habits because we're literally on autopilot every single day.

Take driving, for example. Think about a time when you were driving somewhere, and you arrived at your destination realizing that you didn't even know how you got there, or what you saw along the way. You just got into your car and drove—the same route, the same thoughts, the same patterns, the same stations on the radio, over and over again. It's because you've learned through repetition to drive that same route, so your subconscious literally "takes the wheel" out of habit. It's the very same thing with almost everything we do repeatedly in life.

- They allow feelings to drive their actions, vs. choosing different thoughts that would create the feelings they desire.

Have you ever said to yourself, "I don't feel like it," so you didn't do it? Or, "I'll do that when I feel better," and you rarely feel better, so you don't do anything different than what you've always done. If you're at all like most people, you have been controlled by your feelings, which dictate your actions and reactions to just about every stimuli. The problem is that feelings can be deceptive and are steeped in volatile emotions. Waiting for your feelings to change means you're going to be waiting a very long time. You see, your feelings won't change until your beliefs change first. Stick with me here—by the end of this book you'll have a much deeper understanding of this concept and, more importantly, how to begin rewiring all of this.

- They allow paradigms to keep them stuck where they are.

A simple definition of paradigms is a system of beliefs, ideas, values, and habits that is a way of thinking about the real world. Paradigms aren't always bad, for example, "don't touch the hot stove" or, "I believe people are inherently good," or "seatbelts save lives," etc.

Yet very often, though, we have paradigms that while their purpose is to keep us safe, to resist change, and to protect the status quo, they often diminish us. Thoughts like, "Your life is fine just the way it is—why rock the boat?" or, "Go ahead and eat that extra slice of pizza even if you're full," or "You must have done something to deserve the way he treats you—do better next time." Those are just a few examples of negative paradigms that do not serve us in any healthy way. And these beliefs are *powerful*. Powerful, but NOT invincible! In this book I'll share some tools to help you not only combat what I call this "stinkin' thinkin,'" but help replace that negativity with possibility thinking that will begin to unlock creative ideas for your future that may astound you!

- They believe that someone or something else is responsible for their circumstances, a belief which needlessly and recklessly gives away their power to outside influences.

This is perhaps the most insidious trap of all. Allowing yourself to be defined by what someone else believes to be true is the complete relinquishment of your unique and masterfully crafted humanity. YOU are the highest human authority on you- there is *no one* on earth like you, and that makes you special. When you begin to embrace the concept that you are divinely created, sourced and resourced with infinite potential, *that* is the pivotal moment where your life will begin to shift in ways that YOU create and steer.

Design or Default?

I call the previous scenario a life lived by design- an intentional design that you create and control. The opposite scenario is a life lived by default, where you choose, however subconsciously, to be a victim in your life, tossed about by what happens *to* you vs. choosing what can happen *through* you.

And don't kid yourself, you are either living your life by design *or* default. Both are choices. One serves you; you serve the other. It *is* a choice!

So, what's happening in your life at this moment? If you've never taken an honest assessment of your starting point before, now is the time. Consider these questions:

- Am I living a life by design or default? Do I feel like I'm in the driver's seat or am I stuck in a ditch?
- What areas of my life are causing me the most distress, pain, or even despair right now?
- Is my career going off the rails? Am I on the outs with my boss?
- Do I long to be my own boss? Start my own business?
- Is my home life no longer a haven of safety, sanity, and restoration?
- Am I sick and tired of arguing with everyone closest to me?
- Why am I not taking action with my health? I'm fed up and know I need to make some immediate changes, not

only to get into better shape, but to potentially save my life!

- Have I given up hope that I'll ever find my soul mate?
- Am I a stressed-out business owner strapped by financial obligations I can't meet?
- Am I questioning my purpose in life? I'm being pulled by a deep longing and discontent that there has to be more for me, but I have no idea how to discover what my purpose might be...

Circle of Life Exercise

Here's a simple tool that will help to illustrate the balance—or lack of it—in your life currently. It's called the Circle of Life and is divided into eight sections representing eight key areas that are fundamental aspects of a well-balanced life.

On a scale of 0-10, assume the center of the circle represents 0, meaning you have no satisfaction in that area whatsoever. The outer edge of the circle represents a 10, meaning you have complete satisfaction in that area. So, if every section was completely filled in, the circle would be totally in balance 100%. Note the example shown, which displays a lopsided life where the primary opportunities are in Money, Romantic Relationships, and Friends & Family. The most satisfaction shown in the example is in the areas of Career & Health.

Stop reading now and take a few minutes to complete this exercise with a brutally honest examination of your current level of satisfaction. Think of this as the starting point on your personal journey of transformation, knowing that as you apply the principles and steps you'll learn in this book, you will see your wheel become more and more balanced as you create your life by your own design!

Circle of Life

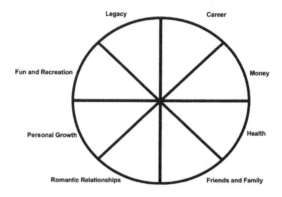

Directions: The eight sections in the Circle of Life represent balance. Feel free to replace any area with something more relevant to you. Regarding the center of the circle as 0 and the outer edge as 10, rank your level of satisfaction with each life area by drawing a straight or curved line to create a new outer edge (see example below). The new perimeter of the circle or wheel represents the Circle of Life. How bumpy would the ride be if this were a real wheel?

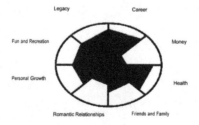

You can scan the QR code for a downloadable copy of the Circle of Life.

So, you're likely saying to yourself at this point, "*Enough* of the pain, Deb! Get to the solution!" I hear you!

And while I can't promise you that after reading this book you'll be promoted, find the love of your life, or become a wildly successful entrepreneur who travels to the south of France every year, I can promise you that there *is* a solution to your current situation, regardless of what that is. And if you'll apply the steps that you'll learn in this book, you *will* have an understanding of multiple paths forward toward those goals, with tools and actions you can apply to move them from possible to probable to predictable!

I'm going to share with you the step-by-step, repeatable process that you can use as a whole, or in parts. WARNING: You may think that this is way too simple to be effective, yet *do not* underestimate the impact these steps can and will have on your life as you make them a regular practice!

Start With Your Owner's Manual

I f you've ever purchased a car, this experience will likely seem familiar to you. I've bought a few vehicles in my lifetime, both new and used, but I get especially excited by the idea of buying a brand-new car. It's the idea of owning something completely new and fresh, the opportunity to be the first to create new experiences and adventures in this vehicle that will take me on exciting journeys.

Every time I've bought a new car, someone from the dealership will go over the basic features, pointing out all the bells and whistles that will enhance my driving experience even further. I vow to explore all of those options on my own...and you know what happens? Almost every single time I revert to using only those options with which I'm already familiar—remember that 95% habit trap I just spoke about?? The vast majority of the time, those extra features never get used because I revert to my comfort zone when driving. And I can tell you that not one single time have I ever read my Owner's Manual, except for when I have a problem. Then it becomes like sacred reading as I know I'll find the answers to what's not working in those pages.

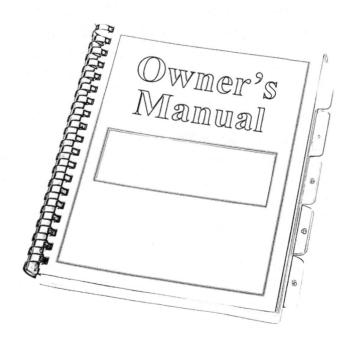

That scenario is very similar to what happens with us as human beings. We walk through life every day with the same routine. We think the same thoughts, feel the same feelings, take the same actions, have the same reactions, and generate the same results! And we wonder why nothing changes!

SAME + SAME + SAME + SAME + SAME = SAME!

We rarely—if ever—take the time to explore our human Owner's Manual—to be curious about *why* we get stuck, about *why* we are frustrated or even desperate. We rarely, if ever, ask ourselves the tough questions about where our disappointing results come from or about why our lives are so unfulfilled. And why we, not unlike our cars, at some point just break down.

We make assumptions that perhaps we're unlucky, or the other person got all the breaks, or believe that life is unfair, and in those limiting assumptions, we continue to create a life by default, devoid of purpose, with a debilitating acceptance of the status quo.

What would change in your life if you understood your own Owner's Manual? What if you could control your internal wiring? What if you could begin creating a life by design, instead of default?
Here's the good news: YOU CAN.

That's why I wrote this book! So, let's begin at the beginning.

Your Operating System

Your Operating System

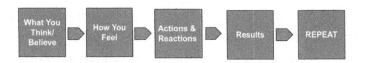

E*verything starts with what you think and what you believe.* Those thoughts generate a vibrational reaction in the body that we recognize as feelings. Those feelings prompt our actions and reactions, and those actions create our results. And as we think about the results we create, we repeat the process over and over again.

Does this sound familiar? If so, you're in great company. What I've described here is the process of how habits get formed. A habit is defined as a regular tendency or practice, one we often don't even think about while we're doing it.

Think again about the example of driving your car. When you first learned to drive, you were probably very aware of what you were doing, your surroundings, other cars, all the elements within the car—the steering wheel, pedals, dashboard, signals, radio, etc. Your senses were on high alert, every thought, every decision deliberate.

Now flash forward to the last time you drove. It's highly likely you didn't even consider most of the details I mentioned in the last paragraph, because your driving is now habitual. All those details that were once so acute have been taken over by your subconscious...as I mentioned previously, you're literally on autopilot most of the time you are driving! Whether it's work, or the grocery store, or your kids' school, or the gym, you probably take the same routes every time you're behind the wheel, not even consciously thinking about what you pass along the way. It's a habit!

Often these habits serve us. We're wired to allow our subconscious to take over small, routine tasks which frees our conscious mind to focus on things requiring our full attention. Yet therein lies the problem.

Almost everything we do on a daily basis requires little-to-no-thought on our part. It's that habit trap fully in place—the "95% autopilot mode"—and yet we wonder why we keep getting the same results over and over and over again. It's as if our brains are on a continual hamster wheel, and what's worse, we're allowing it to happen!

Now let's relate the hamster wheel example to how humans function.

The StickMan

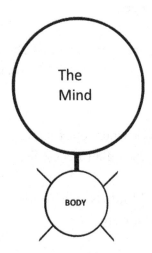

You may recognize this icon from the movie, *The Secret,* and specifically, the contribution from the late brilliant author and lecturer, Bob Proctor. Originally, however, the stick figure illustration is attributed to Dr. Thurman Fleet, a chiropractor and teacher of metaphysics. Dr. Fleet was convinced that often doctors treated only the symptoms instead of the root cause of those symptoms. From that idea, he went on to explore the workings of the mind, which he found to be the origins of our outcomes—the cause of our effects.

Stay with me here—this is a HUGE piece of understanding and harnessing the **7 Surprisingly Simple Steps** you'll learn about shortly. Please don't skip over this!

In this very basic stickman, the larger circle represents the Mind, and the smaller circle represents the body. Our bodies are controlled by our minds—easy to understand so far, right? Let's explore a bit deeper.

In the next stick figure, you'll see that the head, representing the Mind, has been divided into the Conscious Mind and the Subconscious Mind.

The Conscious Mind is where our free will, reasoning, intellect/IQ, and our current level of awareness lie.

The Subconscious Mind is where our beliefs, emotions, memories, and habits are stored.

Here's where this starts to get *really* interesting. As you grasp these next two statements, you'll begin to see the connection between your thoughts and the results you're creating in your life.

The Conscious Mind has the ability to accept, reject, neglect, or create *any* idea. I'm going to repeat that again because the distinction is that important: Your Conscious Mind has the ability to accept, reject, neglect, or create *any* idea.

Now you may not always be able to control what thought or idea pops into your mind to begin with, but you *can* control what you do with that thought or idea. You get to choose.

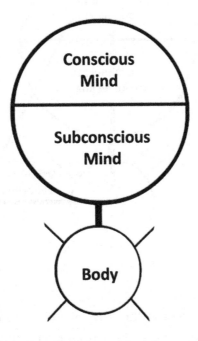

Here is another critical distinction: **Whatever thought the Conscious Mind chooses automatically flows to the Subconscious Mind, which *cannot* choose.** It cannot accept, neglect, reject, or create any thought or idea. **It automatically accepts the chosen thought as FACT and begins to work**

24/7 to turn that thought into reality. That process creates the vibrational energies in our bodies that we recognize as our feelings. Our feelings then motivate our actions (or lack of) as well as our reactions and responses which create our results. See the stick figure below for a representation of this entire cycle:

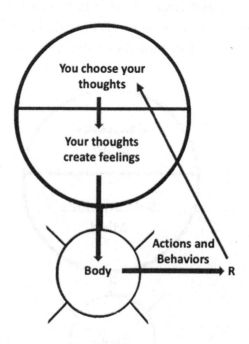

What this represents is the Law of Cause and Effect, which states that for every cause there is an effect, and conversely, for every effect there is a cause. In essence, our thoughts are the initial cause of the eventual effects that show up as our results (represented by the R in the stick figure image).

Take a minute here to look back at your Circle of Life, especially those areas where you have the most discontent and frustration. Ask yourself:

- What specific results am I creating in those areas?
- What do I believe to be true that is contributing to those results?
- What evidence do I have that supports my belief?
- What other root causes could there be that I haven't yet considered?

Let me caution you here. You may be feeling a natural defensiveness to the questions I just posed. Resist that urge. If you're honest with yourself, your current B.S. —your belief system—doesn't serve you well, does it? Otherwise, you likely wouldn't be reading this book. So rather than push back, allow yourself to ask yourself these tough questions, because if you don't take the time to look inward, I can guarantee you that absolutely nothing in your life will change outwardly either. A year from now, ten years from now, you'll be in exactly the same place in your life, and just as unhappy as you are right now. If you're okay with that, stop reading this book and get on with your *Groundhog Day* life.

> *"If you fail to go within, you will go without."*
> ~ Neil Donald Walsch

On the other hand, if you'll honor yourself for a minute, and trust that these questions will help you face some of the root causes of the results you desperately want to change, I can assure you that you will be taking a critical first step in creating a life you love.

Confused? Perhaps even more frustrated? I get it! It will take time and practice to understand this Cause-and-Effect cycle, but I'm going to help break it down for you even more.

This is where your 7 Transformational Steps come into the picture!

The 7 Surprisingly Simple Steps!

Here is an overview:

#1: Amp Your Awareness

#2: Understand Which Circle You're In

#3: Use Your SuperPower!

#4: Source for Solutions

#5: Visualize Your Desired Outcome

#6: Apply Action to Get Traction

#7: Hold Yourself Accountable

Now let's review each one in detail.

STEP #1:

AMP YOUR AWARENESS

The first step may seem like the most obvious, but it's essential. Without it, the other steps are impossible to take.

First, you have to be aware that there is a problem, not unlike the 12 AA steps. You cannot fix something you're not even aware of or refuse to admit exists. Said another way, you can't fix something you won't face.

"What you're aware of, you control. What you're not aware of, controls you."
~ Christian Simpson

If you took the time to answer the questions I asked at the beginning of this book, then you've already stepped up to the painful, yet essential, challenge of taking an honest assessment of your life right now. You see, there was a method to my madness in agitating your pain points because you've already taken the first step in this process—Congratulations!

Because it's so very easy to fall back into old patterns of behavior, let's explore how to stay aware of the traps that pull you right back down into a life lived by default.

Remember when I first talked about how most people are ruled by their feelings? Think of your feelings as an "awareness alert," signaling that a pattern is emerging, either positive, neutral, or negative (or some incremental blend). Obviously, it's the negative feelings that we want to change.

Going back to the stick figure, we learned that our feelings are created by our beliefs which reside in our subconscious—and remember, our subconscious is programmed by the thoughts we consciously choose.

Here's a simple technique for staying aware of what you want to change.

Notice what you're noticing! The next time you have a feeling or thought that doesn't serve you, STOP, and be intentional about noticing it! One of my dear mentors, Mary Morrissey, taught me this simple technique of noticing what I'm paying attention to.

For example, last night before I went to bed, I was feeling a deep sense of disappointment in myself, and I couldn't figure out why. I'd been working hard all day on writing this book and had made significant progress. Yet I was starting to spiral down a rabbit hole of negative self-talk until I began noticing what I was doing! The reason for my stinkin' thinkin' was because I had neglected to exercise yesterday, and I had made a commitment to myself that I would work out five days every single week, and I missed a day. So rather than continue to berate myself for my lack of discipline, I recommitted to get back to my exercise schedule today. And I did.

To help you create a habit of noticing what you're noticing, or as another mentor, Paul Martinelli, calls it, paying attention to what you're paying attention to, find some kind of visual cue to remind you to check in with yourself and your thoughts. For example, Mary used doorknobs as her cue. Every time she saw a doorknob, she would stop for a moment and consider what she was thinking and feeling and noticed any correlation there (go back to the stick figure cycle).

Choose something that you see often—phone, computer, pet, TV, etc. When you see your cue, stop, and ask yourself what you're thinking and how you're feeling, making the intentional connection between the two. The more you repeat this process, the more ingrained it will become. This is an easy, yet very effective tool, to help amp your awareness. Soon, this will become a subconscious habit that positions you to take the NEXT surprisingly simple step to create a life you love!

"Notice what you're noticing!" ~ Mary Morrissey

STEP #2:

UNDERSTAND WHICH CIRCLE YOU'RE IN

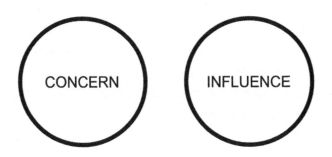

These two circles may look very familiar to you as they were first shared by the brilliant late author, Stephen Covey, in his astoundingly impactful book, *The 7 Habits of Highly Effective People*. I can say without any hyperbole that this book changed my life, particularly these two circles.

These two circles represent where we focus our time and energy. There are things we can change and things, that while we may be concerned about them, we have no ability to change them.

If we're in the circle of concern, we're focused on what we cannot control:

- Weather
- The economy
- Other people's opinions and actions
- Natural disasters
- War
- Price of gas
- Epidemics
- The amount of toilet paper in the store
- Social media
- Your past

In your Circle of Concern are *all the things you cannot do anything about*. The problem is that the vast majority of people spend their time and energy worrying and agonizing about the things they cannot control anyway.

There is a better choice, and that is to invest your precious time and energy in the Circle of Influence. Then you are focused on what you CAN do something about:

- Choosing your thoughts
- Your actions
- Your words
- Your responses and reactions
- Planning for your future
- Taking care of yourself and your family
- Exercising

- Spending time in enriching activities
- Thinking
- Learning
- Evaluating
- Meditating
- ...etc.

Notice that every single thing that falls within the Circle of Influence originates with *you* and *the things you control or influence.* YOU. Not them. YOU.

You've very likely heard of the Serenity Prayer, written by theologian Reinhold Niebuhr. Remembering the words of this prayer is yet another way to stay focused on and in your Circle of Influence:

"God grant me the serenity to accept the things I cannot change;
the courage to change the things I can;
and the wisdom to know the difference."

Stop here and spend some time considering what thoughts occupy your mind most of the time. I've included a simple template for you to use for this exercise, and again I encourage you to proceed with complete honesty about what you are currently thinking and how you're thinking about it. There is *no judgment* here! Later on in this book I'll share another tool about how to think differently in ways that serve you. For now, start creating a snapshot of which circle most reflects your current circumstance.

Primary Thoughts	Circle of Concern	Circle of Influence
Ex: Price of Gas	✓	
Ex: I want to be healthier		✓

Download your own exercise: Which Circle Am I In?

When I first read *The 7 Habits of Highly Effective People,* I was blown away by the knowledge that I didn't have to live my life subject to how I felt. I didn't have to be affected by other people's negative opinions and destructive actions. I learned that I didn't have to feel bad or sad or disappointed or embarrassed or hopeless or any other of a thousand different debilitating emotions that seemed to rule my life at the time.

I learned I had a choice. And this brings us to the 3rd surprisingly simple step.

STEP #3:

USE YOUR SUPERPOWER!

My husband, Patrick, is a Marvel/DC movie fanatic. I don't think there's a superhero movie released in the last 25 years that he hasn't seen. This means there aren't many that I haven't seen either, what with my attempt to be a supportive wife! It's certainly fun to entertain the idea of being invisible, being able to fly, or having the power of mind control, etc.

Yet even though none of us are superheroes in that respect, we all do indeed possess a superpower, perhaps the most underappreciated and underutilized of them.

If you've been paying attention, you'll have noticed that I've mentioned this superpower multiple times throughout this book already.

Choice Is Your SuperPower!® I trademarked that phrase for a reason. It's been estimated that we make an average of *35,000 choices every single day!* Think about that for a minute! We make almost 300 choices about food alone! Now when you layer on the studies showing that up to 95% of what we do daily we don't even think about, you start to get an understanding of how many choices we make subconsciously every day as well. Choices that we make out of habit, choices that are impacting our results in ways that don't serve us, choices that keep us stuck in a life lived by default, not design.

Yet they are choices. And those choices have consequences.

Let's go back to the two circles for a minute.

When you are aware (Step 1) of what you're thinking—noticing what you're noticing—you are in an objective space in your thinking. You are aware that there are options- to move into your circle of concern *or* to move into your circle of influence.

Think about this for a minute: When you're in this space where you are noticing what you're noticing, you are observing your thoughts and feelings objectively—without judgment. It's this objectivity that allows you to engage your superpower!

Let me tell you a brief but powerful true story that illustrates this point.

Back during World War II, there was a man named Viktor Frankl who was a highly respected psychiatrist in his native Austria before he was captured and taken to the Auschwitz prison camp. There he was subjected to repeated torture, taunting, and other unspeakable inhuman acts. Yet it was in this unimaginable circumstance that Frankl came to the realization that, regardless of what the Nazis did to him physically, they could never take control of his mind, his mindset. It was from this horror that he eventually made a decision that resulted in this famous quote:

"In between stimulus and response there is a space. In that space is our power to choose our response. In our response lies our growth and our freedom." ~ Viktor Frankl

The vast majority of us will never experience anything as nightmarish as what Frankl went through, yet we continually give up the gift of choice as we go mindlessly about our existence day after day, subconsciously caught up in the habits of our life that keep us stuck.

So, when something happens to you (stimulus) and *before* you respond, savor that objective space because *this* is where your life can change *dramatically* and virtually immediately. *This* is where your SUPERPOWER enters the picture!

Remember that CHOICE is your SuperPower!® Before you make your choice, consider some of these questions:

- What is my best option here?
- What choice serves me?
- What choice best serves other people?
- What choice moves me forward?

- What are the consequences if I react vs. respond?
- When I've made this same choice in the past, what was the result?
- What would my best self do here?
- If I think about where I'd like to be a year from now, five years from now, what would that version of me do right now?

On the next page I've included a graph and an exercise, showing the options of typical unproductive responses as well as more empowering ones. There are several blank rows for you to consider your current situation—how are you responding? How is that working for you? What other, more positive options could you consider?

Practice this! Begin to discipline yourself to *pause* when something happens. Pause and consider that objective space where you can exercise your SuperPower *before* you respond or react. I guarantee you that as you put this exercise into consistent practice, you'll be amazed at how your life begins to transform. *I guarantee it!*

You could choose to:

Option	Better Option?
Shut down	Be curious
Retaliate	Reflect
Get angry	Ask yourself how that serves you
Quit	Find a different solution
Keep talking	Listen
Judge	Respect
Blame	Accept responsibility
Sit on the couch eating bonbons	Go for a hike
Stay stuck where you are	Explore what ignites your soul

At this point you may be thinking that this is all starting to make sense, but it may seem overwhelming. You may be feeling tempted to give up and just accept your life the way it is—it's too hard to change!

I understand. Again, you're not alone in those feelings.

Yet I implore you to stay with the deeper feeling of longing and discontent. *Lean into it,* because that's your spirit, your intuition, prompting you to at least give yourself a chance—a chance to explore a life that you create, that you've dreamed about, that would fill you with purpose and possibility. Aren't you worth that? The answer to that is a resounding YES!

It doesn't matter who you are, or where you're from, or what you've done or not done. You deserve to live a life you love!

Would you like some support as you create your new life? Consider the opportunity to work directly with me one-on-one to provide the structure and framework you'll need to break old habits, stop your stinkin' thinkin', get unstuck, and create a life you love. Scan the QR overleaf to schedule a discovery call with me.

I don't have the time or the bandwidth to work with everyone as a VIP Client. Yet I find this Coach/Client collaboration to be so rewarding for both parties that I carve out time to work with a handful of seriously committed people for 6-12 months and longer if necessary.

Why at least six months? Because it's taken you a lifetime to create the thinking, beliefs, habits, behaviors, and results that are the source of your pain. It will take time to break them and to build new, sustainable, energizing, transforming thoughts and beliefs. If you choose to work with me in this supportive partnership, it will be much more likely that you'll create the results you so long for.

Still interested? Are you willing to make the time, do the work, and make the investment required? If you're still answering YES! then scan the QR code below to schedule your call with me: Book a Discovery Call with Deb.

Let's move on to the 4th surprisingly simple step.

STEP #4:

SOURCE FOR SOLUTIONS

Now that you've discovered the objective space where you can choose your response, you're in the right mindset to begin ideating on what you'd love to create in your life. Instead of reacting automatically, you're learning to be intentional about your choices.

Sourcing for ideas is a great place to start thinking about solutions, possibilities, and ideas. I've used the exercise you're about to learn multiple times, and it never fails to astonish me at what transpires. It's in this step that you'll begin to appreciate that you DO have genius within you!

It's absolutely critical that you enter into this exercise in the right environment and with the right mindset. Essentially what is happening at its core is the organic connection generated between you and Source. The fabulous, late Wayne Dyer said,

"If prayer is us talking to God, then intuition is God talking to us."

Regardless of what you call this Source—God, Spirit, the Divine, etc.—it is a level of intelligence far greater than your intellect, and you will experience an undeniable creative connection that you'll be tapping into when you authentically enter into this step.

Read through all these steps before you begin, and *remain open-minded.*

Here's the process:

- Find a quiet place where you will be uninterrupted for at least 5-10 minutes, minimum.
- Open your mind to the Source of all ideas and inspiration. It's where your intuition comes from.
- Decide in advance that *all* productive ideas are welcome. (Remember, you have a choice!)

- Begin with an intelligent question specific to your interest/desire/dream/goal/next step to start the process. NOTE: "Why" questions are typically "low amperage" questions because your intellect will look for logical, already-known ideas. Instead, try "what" questions, as they tap into a Source greater than your own intellect. "What" questions invite "what's possible" options and solutions.

  Examples:
    - O "What can I do in the next two weeks that will generate at least five business Clients within the next 60 days?
    - O "If I could do anything in life as a source of income generation, what would I do?"
    - O "What am I most passionate about?"
    - O "What steps can I take to begin creating a sense of self-acceptance, self-confidence, and the belief that I am *more* than enough, just the way I am?"
    - O "What is one step I can take to explore starting my own business?"
    - O "What step(s) can I take in the next 30 days that will generate the revenue (be specific on the amount) needed to create breathing room in my business and personal life?

You get the idea! Start with a burning question that creates an energetic reaction within you. That's a great place to begin!

- Now you're ready to begin sourcing. Write down literally *every single idea* that pops into your head as a result of the question you asked. Do not edit or judge any idea! Stopping to judge, or even to think about what ideas are flowing will stop or significantly interrupt your energy flow. You'll have ample time at the end of this step to review and evaluate the validity of any/all ideas. *Keep writing!* Write until you have no more ideas and your well has been fully tapped!
- Once you're done, review your list! You now have a bundle of ideas to help get you started on creating a life you love!

Note: The Sourcing exercise alone is a powerful one, and it *does* work as you continue to invest your time and brain power to the practice of idea generation. If you want to explore how to fully maximize the entire process, there are four more steps that will expand the impact of this exercise even further. Purchase the full PDF blueprint here:

The 5-Step Blueprint to Find Your Passion and Create a Life You Love!

Original Photo on Unsplash

STEP #5:

VISUALIZE YOUR OUTCOME

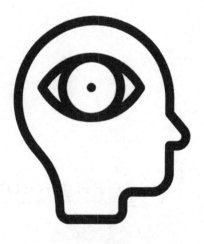

With the completion of Step 4, you now likely have multiple ideas and possible steps to begin moving you toward your goals and dreams. Step 5 moves the ideas and solutions into the production part of the process.

Our minds are the most powerful creative engines in the universe. Every single thing that exists was a thought before it became a thing. That means that before you can create what you'd love to have in your life, you have to first imagine it.

Consider this—our brains think in pictures, not words. For example, if I say the word "bed" to you, what pops into your head? It's certainly not the letters, B-E-D is it? No! You probably pictured your own bed, perhaps wooden or wrought iron, a bedspread, quilt, or blanket of some sort, probably even the color of the bedspread. If you're like me, you have about 15 pillows on the bed of all different sizes and shapes, some for comfort, some for decor, much to my husband Patrick's chagrin... ("why do you need more than one pillow at a time?!?").

As you think about what you'd love to create in your life, this imagery is critical. It engages the right side of your brain as well as your left. The more specific you can be in your mind's eye, the more detail it has to begin transferring the thought to reality.

This powerful process is called *visualization*, and many of the most successful people on the planet use this technique. One of the most well-known stories of visualization is that of actor and comedian, Jim Carrey. When Carrey first arrived as a complete unknown in Hollywood back in 1990, he wrote himself a check for $10M dated five years in the future, and put in the subject line, "for acting services rendered." He put the check in his pocket, and often retrieved it to visualize what he would do with the money once he cashed the check. He did this so often that the paper check began to deteriorate. He would be driving somewhere and think about all the things he wanted to attain and achieve in his life and would say to himself, "I DO have all these things—they're out there—I just haven't gotten them yet."

And, of course, Jim Carrey DID indeed get his $10M payday in 1995 when he made the movie, *Dumb and Dumber* (Ironic!). He even inspired Oprah Winfrey to become a visualization practitioner, and of course, she's been highly successful in her own right as well.

> *"If you can see it, and believe it, it's a lot easier to achieve it!"* ~ Oprah Winfrey

I've had multiple positive experiences with visualization in many forms, and I'll share a couple of them here to help you get started.

My first exposure to this exercise was with one of my Coaches and mentors who I've mentioned a few times already in this book, Mary Morrissey. Mary had us engage in a practice called "Time Machine." We would break out into groups of two where we would "travel ahead in time three years" and describe to our partners exactly what was happening in our lives at that future time. We used language as if our goals and dreams had already happened, using present tense verbiage, such as "I AM_____" and "I HAVE_____" to describe what was happening or had happened.

The more we engaged in the Time Machine exercise, the more specific our descriptions would become, so this isn't a one-and-done exercise. Repetition helps to anchor the picture in our minds, giving our goal-seeking organism—our subconscious—ample material to work with to begin creating our new reality.

Note: This works to create negative outcomes as well. By that I mean that if you aren't happy with the results you're creating in your life, ask yourself what kind of mind pictures you're starting with…it's the same with words and thoughts (go back to the stick figure cycle). Junk in equals junk out.

The most recent experience I've had with the visualization exercise was just a few weeks ago. This time, I wrote a letter from my future self to my current self, describing what was happening in my life five years in the future. Here's a snapshot of what I wrote:

Dear Deb,

I'm sitting in the office of my dream home in San Diego, overlooking the Pacific Ocean. My office is at the corner of the house. Two of the four walls are all glass, 20 feet high, with panoramic views of the ocean (my happy place!). The other two walls are filled with floor-to-ceiling books (my dream library), and it's here that I spend most of my time being inspired, relaxing in a comfortable, plush chocolate leather club chair. Patrick and I have over 500 books of all sorts—biographies, history, novels, art/art history, business, personal investment, etc. Even though we donate books every year to the local library, we seem to continue to acquire more. It's our favorite pastime!

When we're not in the library, we spend lots of time out on the 50 x 50 ft. deck, which has a lounging area, built-in kitchen with gas grill, small pool/hot tub, and built-in fire pit. It's here that we enjoy great wine with great conversation, while taking in the spectacular view of downtown San Diego and the ocean. Life is so good!

As it's September, Patrick and I are packing to leave for our trip to Europe as we do every year, with one to two months away. Our first stop is a month in Italy (my favorite place to travel), where we'll stay in a VRBO in Sorrento and base from there. We're celebrating our 31st anniversary and have never been happier!

As I sit at my six-foot glass and ebony wood desk, I am writing this letter of gratitude to thank you for committing to your vision and mission of helping others transform their lives so many years ago. I want to thank you for using your SuperPower to choose to play BIG, even when you didn't have all the answers or know every step of the journey. You stepped out in faith—and kept taking the steps you could take, and look at the results!

This letter goes on for several pages, and ever since I first wrote it, I continue to revisit and rewrite it, being more specific and focused each time. The repetition and refinement continue to sharpen the images in my mind and it's powerful!

Now it's your turn. Take some time before you read further to explore this visualization exercise for your life. Think about what you'd love to create in the key areas of your life: Health, Relationships/Romance, Vocation/Career, Freedom with Time and Money, Spirituality, and Legacy. If your life could be anything you could imagine, what would that look like? This will be an ideation experience, just like with Step 4: Sourcing. Let the ideas flow. Don't edit. Write until you literally cannot think of another idea. Then go back, and read what you wrote. Note the connection between those words/images and your feelings/emotions (stick figure guy again!).

You have just created the very first step in making your dreams a reality. Revisit and rewrite often—at least weekly. Repetition is the first law of learning and by doing so, you are anchoring the details in your mind's eye. Your vision will sharpen every time you engage in this creative process.

Visualization helps you to wire your vision. Step 6 will help you fire it! (And by "fire" I mean ignite, not terminate!)

STEP #6:

APPLY ACTION TO GET TRACTION!

Without action applied to the previous five steps, all you've got is a movie in your head. NOTHING happens until you take the steps you *can* take.

Your next step is to act on your ideas—to honor them, to fully serve them through your planning, execution, and evaluation of each step of your goal and dream.

Looking back on the ideated lists you created from Steps 4 & 5, what are the most important steps? When will you take them? Specifically, are they prioritized and scheduled on your calendar? If not, stop, and do this before proceeding.

Let's get strategic and specific here. Up to this point, you've identified multiple ideas that can move you forward to creating a life you love. Now you're going to start anchoring those ideas with specifics and priorities.

Following are several action commitments to lock down as you get started building your strategic plan. You'll notice my intentional use of the term, "burning desire," taken directly from Napoleon Hill's brilliant classic, *Think and Grow Rich*. This is another book that should be part of your permanent—and repeatedly read—library (along with *7 Habits* already mentioned in Step 2).

Hill defines a burning desire as an obsession, a definite "keen pulsating desire" that transcends everything. It's not a want or hope or wish; it's so much bigger than that! The greater your burning desire and your commitment to it, the greater the likelihood that you will act on it, moving that desire from possible to probable to eventually predictable!

STRATEGIC PLANNING

My #1 Goal/Dream/Burning Desire (be specific):

I will achieve my Goal/Dream/Burning Desire by (date):

This Goal/Dream/Burning Desire is important to me because (purpose):

This Goal/Dream/Burning Desire, once accomplished, will add value to others by (it benefits more than just me):

I will know I have achieved my Goal/Dream/Burning Desire when (how is this achievement measurable):

The immediate actions I KNOW I can take to manifest my Goal/Dream/Burning Desire are (action is required!):

The dates/times I have added into my calendar/schedule to ensure I am serving my Goal/Dream/Burning Desire are (when are you taking action):

DO NOT skip this last step! Schedule the actions in your calendar. Take the steps you know you *can* take, with where you are right now, with what you have right now.

You don't have to know every step along the path to create what you'd love to have in your life! This is where many people get discouraged and quit before they even get started! They believe they have to know HOW to get from here to there, and that's just not realistic. Why not? Because if you knew how you'd already be doing it!

As your awareness increases, as you become more insightful and intuitive as to what's possible, as you believe more and more in your creative abilities, you will find that new steps, new ideas, and new possibilities present themselves.

Think about hiking or climbing a mountain. At the base of the mountain your view looks one way. You can see things from the valley floor, and you might even be able to look up and see the mountain top, but your view is limited. Yet as you climb the mountain, your view changes. The higher you climb, the more you can see. It's the same way with your Goals/Dreams/ Burning Desires!

Trust the process and keep taking the steps you CAN take— and keep taking them!

STEP #7:

HOLD YOURSELF ACCOUNTABLE TO YOU!

L eadership expert, John C. Maxwell, says, "Experience isn't the best teacher. Evaluated experience is!" His point is that experience alone is no guarantee that you'll learn from that experience, which is why so many people keep making the same mistakes over and over again. A much more effective approach is to take time to learn from your experiences and apply that learning in the future.

How do you do that?

What will you do differently in the future?

Take time regularly—ideally every single day—to reflect on what's happened throughout that day. Ask yourself these questions:

- What were my successes?
  (And I guarantee that you had some! Recognize that even little wins count. Little wins make a difference. You don't have to hit a home run every single time you're at bat. Compiled base hits—or even walks—will score runs as well. Count the small stuff—it matters!)
- What were the opportunities or challenges? What didn't work the way I intended? (Notice that I didn't say "failures." In my opinion, failures are only failures when there is no movement forward, no learning, no reflection, no benefit that resulted from the experience.)
- What happened during my day that I'd like to change? How would I change it?
  What good can come from this disappointment? These are all very healthy, very powerful questions to ask yourself that, when the answers are applied, will move you forward in a way that fuels your future.
- What can/will I do differently going forward?
- What am I saying to myself to reaffirm my commitments to myself and in who I am right now? How am I expressing appreciation and patience for who I am becoming?

- What is happening in my life for which I'm grateful? (Focusing on what you already have in your life has immense benefits and will help to shift your perspective about what's important.)

I have a tool that can help you with this daily exercise. It's called a Gratitude Journal and it's a 30-day, electronic, evergreen tool that you can use over and over again.

Get your Gratitude Journal via the QR code below.

Taking time daily to reflect on the important things in your life and expressing gratitude for those things is a healthy habit to build—for learning, insight, application, and personal growth.

There are significant and multiple benefits to building a daily "Attitude of Gratitude" including:

- Gratitude improves your brain and physical health.
- Gratitude creates happiness.

- Gratitude helps you sleep better.
- Gratitude is the antidote to toxic emotions—you CANNOT have a spirit of gratitude and worry or be bitter at the same time!
- Gratitude improves relationships.
- Gratitude opens the door to people and opportunities.
- Gratitude is the evidence of maturity.
- Gratitude connects us with the ultimate Source of all things.

This 44-page journal is easy to use and will not require a lot of your time. It is designed to be used daily over a 30-day period. The pages are formatted with inspiring quotes throughout and inset with space for you to record your thoughts on gratitude, successes, and affirmations. At the end of each week and month you'll see several blank pages designed for your reflection regarding what you've learned about yourself and your journey, and to place you in a mindset to channel those learnings into continuing to create the life you love!

As this journal is electronic, you can replenish each month, or even begin to add your own favorite quotes and ideas, or you can just print and reuse as is. Most important is building the daily discipline of taking moments of quiet reflection to invest in your most important asset—you!

Overleaf is a sample page from the Gratitude Journal.

This Journal is designed to be used daily over a 30-day period. The pages are formatted with inspiring quotes throughout and inset with space for you to record your thoughts on Gratitude, Successes, and Affirmations.

Here is an example of what this might look like: Note that using 'I AM' statements are some of the most powerful, as you are 'acting as if' you already ARE the person in your statement, even if you don't feel that way, or that may not yet be your circumstance. Words create. Use present-tense words/phrases intentionally. Through repetition, you will begin to create a life you love!

GRATITUDE:
• *I am thankful for the kindness of others when I need it most*
• *I am thankful for the new job lead I found today*
• *I am thankful for my workout coach who believes in me, even when she's torturing me!*
• *I am thankful for my husband who is an amazing cook- Homemade pasta tonight!*
• *I am thankful for my pets who love me unconditionally*

SUCCESSES:
• *I completed one chapter in the book I'm writing*
• *Someone I've coached in the past just got a promotion today- I am proud!*
• *I handled a difficult conversation with a peer today and we resolved our issue*
• *I made healthy food choices all day today!*
• *I reconnected with an old friend who I haven't spoken to in a long time*

AFFIRMATIONS:
• *I know that I am more than I sometimes realize because the power that created and breathes me is within me*
• *My past does not define me- I am creating a different ending to my story*
• *I am more than my circumstances*
• *I am a unique and wonderfully created Child of God*
• *I am making today so amazing that tomorrow will be jealous!*

At the end of each week and at the end of the month you'll see several blank pages designed for your reflection over what you've learned about yourself and your journey, and to place you in a mindset to channel those learnings into continuing to *Create the Life You Love!*

You can access your complimentary Gratitude Journal by scanning the QR code.

In addition to your daily reflection, I highly encourage a formal weekly recap as well. The Franklin Covey organization created another tool that has helped me immensely with my weekly reflection, refining, and refocusing. It's called a weekly WIG meeting—where you reflect on your Wildly Important Goal. I learned this approach many years ago, and I still have a weekly WIG meeting with myself! Here are some thoughts and questions to ponder during your weekly Goal/Dream/Burning Desire/WIG meeting:

- Review the commitments and priorities you set from the previous week.

  - What was my MAIN priority? Think Goals/ Dreams/Burning Desires here...
  - What actions did I take to ensure the Main Thing stayed the Main Thing?
  - What worked? Why did it work? What will I carry forward into the coming week?

○ What didn't work? Why didn't it work? What actions didn't I take that I scheduled? If they were priorities, what got in the way? Are they still viable and if so, carry them forward into next week's schedule.

○ What were the big wins?

○ How will I improve in the coming week?

○ What new ideas do I have as a result of my ever-increasing awareness that I should consider as a priority?

○ What are my ongoing priorities?

○ What specific actions will I take next week?

○ What habits am I focused on breaking? How will I break them next week?

○ What habits am I focused on building? How will I build them next week?

• Next, SCHEDULE your top priority actions before you schedule anything else!

Here's a tip to consider when scheduling the action(s) that support your Main Thing. What is the most productive time of day for you? When are you at your best? If you're a morning person, schedule your most important activities in the morning. Conversely, if you're a night owl, work in the evening. I get that your schedule may not be completely your own. You may have meetings, other work commitments, family obligations, etc. that require specific time on your calendar. But you DO have autonomy with some of your time, probably more than you're even aware of. Use that autonomous time to focus on your top priorities, and align the time when you are at your peak.

And don't allow yourself to be distracted by Shiny Object Syndrome! Hey, we've all been there and are vulnerable to S.O.S. when we lose sight of our Burning Desire! To help me stay focused, I have this huge note taped to my computer:

DOES THIS DISTRACTION MOVE ME IN THE DIRECTION OF MY MAIN THING FASTER OR IN A MORE VALUABLE WAY? IF NOT, WHY AM I DOING IT?

I've found this to be a helpful reminder to keep my focus on my Main Thing!

Last, I strongly encourage you to find an accountability partner. Because while you may be fired up and focused right now, what is likely to happen is that you will get lulled right back into your comfort zone. Most people do. It's what's familiar to you. Remember that you have a lifetime of BS—a lifetime of a Belief System, that, up until now, hasn't served you well, or else you likely wouldn't be reading this book. Until you've broken those old habits and replaced them with new, healthy, energizing, and creative ones and sustained them over a period of time, you *will* revert back to what you've always done in the past!

Your Comfort Zone is Your BIGGEST Dream-Killer!

By aligning yourself with an accountability partner, you have a ready-made safeguard to help you stay on track to the commitments you've made to YOU!

This person should be someone who can boldly speak truth to you, who will call you out when you need it, and who will help to get you back on track when you go off the rails or begin to feel discouraged.

And it will happen! You *will* hear those paradigms—that stinkin' thinkin'—start to tell you all the reasons why you should revert back to your comfort zone. You'll hear the voices of doubt telling you that you should get your head out of the clouds, stay where you are—after all, who do you think you are to even begin to attempt to make your dreams come true? Who are you, Cinderella? Trust me, it will happen!

Anytime you are making changes in your life, especially significant ones as you're doing with these 7 Steps, your old paradigms will try to preserve the status quo. On one hand, you can think of this as a sign that you are indeed moving in the direction of your dreams! On the other hand, it's very easy to succumb to those old voices! After all, isn't that what you've done your whole life?

This is why an accountability partner can be so vital in helping you stay accountable to yourself and the commitments you're making to create a life you love!

SUCCESS STORIES

At the very beginning of this book, I stated that I've seen these steps work in the transformation of thousands of lives, and I'm going to share just a few of those success stories with you in this chapter.

Note: These are all REAL Clients of mine with real problems and very real successes! I've changed their names to protect confidentiality. You'll notice that I'm again using the acronym S.O.S., but instead of it being Shiny Object Syndrome, I'm flipping that now to signify Situation Outcome Solution! And yes, there's a reason why I'm sharing the outcome before the solution.

Case Study #1 BREAKING THROUGH BARRIERS: REBECCA

SITUATION:

When Rebecca first came to me, she was frustrated from being stagnant in her career. She'd been in the same role with the same company for over a decade yet wanted to take on greater responsibility that would better utilize her skills and positively impact the organization. Rebecca was working insane hours, which was negatively impacting her health as well as her relationship with her husband. Rebecca believed she was deserving of an executive promotion but didn't know what else to do or how to break through the barriers in her life. She was stuck.

OUTCOME:

Now, after I have been working with Rebecca for several months, she is being groomed for a promotion and her confidence is building to the point that she can effectively engage with the C-Suite executives—soon to be her coworkers. She is even taking some much needed and deserved time off to travel with the love of her life—yes, it's her husband!

SOLUTION:

So how did Rebecca create such change in her life?

Her first step was to identify her longer-term goals, to determine what was most important to her in her life (the MAIN THING!) and then begin to build backwards. As author Stephen Covey describes in the *7 Habits* book, Rebecca began with the end in mind and created a strategic, step-by-step action plan to get promoted and to spend more time with her husband.

Second, she analyzed where she was spending all her time using a simple tool called the 15-Minute Miracle. Through that exercise she discovered that she had lost sight of her priorities and was caught up in reacting vs. being proactive. She also used some of the strategic planning tools I've shared with you and began aligning her actions with her values.

Last, as her awareness of what was possible increased, along with her confidence and strategic thinking, she applied those new-found abilities to thinking more globally about how to influence her company, and the C-Suite noticed. As I write this book her promotion is imminent.

Case Study #2 SKYROCKETING SELF-CONFIDENCE: EUGENE

SITUATION:

Like so many people, Eugene was suffering from crippling self-doubt when we first began working together. This doubt kept him stuck in a dead-end routine at work where he purposely tried to fly under the radar. He believed that if he kept his head down and did his job well, that people would leave him alone. He felt he didn't fit in anywhere. He believed he wasn't as smart, or articulate, or as polished as most people. He felt he was constantly being judged by others, and it was demoralizing. Eugene felt like he had no sense of direction or purpose for his life. He was sinking fast.

OUTCOME:

Eugene and I have worked together for several years now, and his entire life has changed. He has clearly defined his life's purpose and passion and has created a plan to get his advanced degree in a completely different field than the one in which he is now working. Ironically, he's received a promotion at work that is providing the income he needs to get through school and onto his dream. He is a go-to expert in his new role, and is being encouraged to take on even more responsibility, even though his passions lie elsewhere. On a personal note, Eugene found his soulmate and is engaged to be married. Eugene credits these principles, as well as our Coaching relationship, with this incredible turnaround in his life!

SOLUTION:

The most important step in Eugene's success was in understanding his Owner's Manual, his personal operating system. He immediately grasped how the Law of Cause and Effect was controlling his life and changed the input—his thinking—which changed his beliefs about himself (cause). He learned to flip the script on his stinkin' thinkin' that allowed him to rewrite an entirely different powerful internal script about his abilities, and his confidence soared! With his skyrocketing self-esteem, Eugene identified what his true passions were, and he believed he could make those passions his reality. Last, Eugene committed to—and took the necessary action steps that would test this new thinking—his rewired operating system. He's applied this thinking—it's not new for him anymore—to successfully and dramatically shift what he believed to be possible in his life, and the results (effects) continue to exceed his expectations!

Case Study #3 UNLEASHING HER INNER GENIUS: LESLIE

SITUATION:

When Leslie first became my Client, she had just taken on an expanded role at work and was looking for some executive coaching. She was challenged with building cooperative relationships with some of her peer group and senior leadership because she purposely held herself back in meetings and even in hallway conversations because she didn't want to appear confrontational. She continually second-guessed herself and was beginning to believe that she was in over her head with her scope of responsibilities and the need to work cross-collaboratively. Her once rock-solid confidence plummeted along with her career aspirations, and she had resigned herself to believe that where she was in her career was as good as it was going to get.

OUTCOME:

Leslie and I are still working together, so her ultimate story is yet to unfold. I can tell you that she has created some amazing turnarounds at work. She's now a sought-after speaker on and off campus and is frequently asked to plan and host executive meetings and presentations. Leslie has gained tremendous insight into how to create win-win relationships both at work and in her personal life. In a very short period of time, Leslie has been given significantly more responsibility, adding two additional major Clients for the company as well as taking on a dozen new direct reports. She's gotten an off-cycle bump in salary, a new title, and is even writing a book!

SOLUTION:

There was a multi-pronged approach to Leslie's initial success, a combination of leadership coaching and mentoring, the application of DISC tools and exercises, and speaking classes that certainly played a role in many of her outcomes. That said, the most powerful tool by far was the knowledge and insight Leslie gained through the coaching process. That awareness led her to the discovery that she does indeed have genius within her. She realized that she has the answers and solutions to the questions in her life, but just hadn't known how to tap into that inner resource. Like all my clients, Leslie came into the coaching relationship with an open mind and willing spirit, ready to invest in herself and in the future she longed for. It was in the spirit of authenticity and transparency that Leslie was able to think deeply into the questions being asked that challenged her BS— her old Belief System that wasn't serving her. She worked hard on crushing the paradigms that didn't serve her by repeatedly flipping the negative script and replacing it with empowering, genius-unleashing beliefs. Leslie is creating her success story page by page, chapter by chapter.

My Success Story

Lastly, and very briefly, I will share with you that these principles have helped me not only to experience great success during my retail career, but also to rebound when that career collapsed. Within a span of several years, two of my executive roles were eliminated, I was virtually flat broke, all my retirement funds were depleted, and I was starting over from scratch.

Yet I knew there was more in store for my life. And I knew these principles worked! I am a living testimony that you CAN create a life you love! In the few short years since hitting rock bottom, I have started my own thriving company, moved to the beautiful state of Utah with my beloved husband, Patrick, am traveling the world, and am happier and more fulfilled than I've ever been!

These are just a few of the thousands of success stories I have been fortunate enough to be a part of over these past 30 years. Perhaps you see yourself in Rebecca's, Eugene's, and Leslie's stories. Or perhaps you've been where I was and feel that you've hit your own rock bottom. If so, you should know that there IS a path for you. You, too, can become a success story in your own life!

A GREAT place to start is to reread this book, take notes, complete the exercises, and consistently take the 7 Surprisingly Simple Steps!

Here they are once again:

#1: Amp Your Awareness

#2: Understand Which Circle You're In

#3: Use Your SuperPower!

#4: Source for Solutions

#5: Visualize Your Desired Outcome

#6: Apply Action to Get Traction

#7: Hold Yourself Accountable

I can tell you that, even though I've been studying and teaching these steps for many years, I still learn something new every time I review them. It's not that the principles have changed— they were solid years ago and will be years from now. What has changed is my awareness. I'm in a different place in my continually evolving life. New insights and ideas leap out at me. It's just like the mountain-climbing example I shared—as you climb higher, your view changes. Wayne Dyer said it so well:

"When you change the way you look at things,
the things you look at change!"

NEXT STEPS

I f you've purchased this book, and have read it up to this page, congratulations! You are one of a select group of people who are genuinely curious about how to create a life you love. You should be proud that you've come this far in challenging your current beliefs about what is possible in and for your life!

So where do you go from here? I will say in complete transparency that simply reading a book will do nothing but engage your mind for a short period of time, and then you'll go back to your comfort zone, *unless* you take action consistently that moves you in the direction of your goals/dreams/burning desires.

If you commit to consistently and authentically following the 7 Surprisingly Simple Steps outlined in this book, you will shift your thinking, which will impact your beliefs (cause), that will change how you feel, and as a result, you'll take different actions and respond differently as well. As you engage your SuperPower of Choice, you will also begin to create results (effects) that you are longing for.

That IS why you bought this book, right?

Yet many of you will find that you need additional structure, support, guidance, etc. to help you as you do the work of the work. Breaking old habits of thinking and behavior is hard work, and even those with the most determined discipline may find it hard not to slip back into the dangerous, dream-killing comfort zone.

> *"Men are anxious to improve circumstances, but never willing to improve themselves; they therefore remain bound."* ~ James Allen

Why Work with a Coach?

There is no question that authentic Coaching is one of the most transformational relationships on the planet, because it's one of the only interactions that impacts at the conscious AND subconscious levels.

As you learned in Step #1: Amp Your Awareness, it's your subconscious that stores your belief system, your habits, your paradigms, your emotions. And because they are subconscious, you aren't actively thinking about what serves you, and what doesn't. It's that habit trap! Without an intention to challenge your BS, your belief system, you will by habit revert to your comfort zone and your thoughts, beliefs, actions, and reactions will stay the same. And consequentially, your results will stay the same!

"The quality of your life is determined by the quality of the questions you ask yourself." ~Tony Robbins

I would add to Tony's quote: The quality of your life is determined by the quality of the questions you ask yourself or that you allow someone else to ask you. Coaching is so powerful because of the intuitive questions an authentic Coach will ask that require you to dig deep—to that subconscious level. It's there that you will *shake up* what you have always believed to be true or possible about yourself and your life. It's there that you will replace those limiting beliefs with genius-unleashing beliefs. It's in this relationship that you will awaken to the infinite potential that lies within you—that same potential that lies within every human being on this beautiful blue globe.

How to explore working with me:

At this point, you may want to explore working with me in a Coach/Client relationship. As I mentioned before, the investment is not for everyone. However, as I also mentioned, I have reserved specific time in my calendar to work with a handful of committed one-on-one Clients because the Coaching relationship is so rewarding. It's truly one of the most profound and impactful experiences for both my Clients and me. If you'd like to explore this partnership, overleaf is a link that will take you to my calendar where you can schedule a discovery call at a time that works for you.

As of this book release, there is a financial investment for the discovery call which will be applied to any Coaching package with me. Once you schedule your call time, you'll be asked to answer a few questions that will help me to prepare for our conversation.

Still interested? Great! Here is the QR code to my calendar to get started:

You can choose the life you've led up until now. But ask yourself, how's that working out for you?

Ultimately your next step is up to you. You can choose to believe that you have vast potential that is as of yet unfulfilled. You can choose to believe that you DO have the power to create a life you love. You can choose to believe in YOU.

You DO get to choose, you know...

Choice Is Your SuperPower!

Choose wisely!

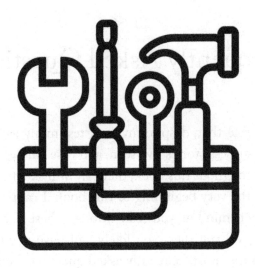

In the Appendix/Resources section of this book, I have compiled the tools referenced in several chapters. You'll also see additional courses, webinars, and workshops that you can access which will help you to stay focused on your journey. I encourage you to explore these resources, many of which are complimentary.

Frequently Asked Questions

I can imagine that, despite my own testimony as well as the years of success stories I've seen, and case studies I've shared with you throughout this book, there are still skeptics out there. I get it. At the very beginning of this book, I cautioned you to keep an open mind as you read through these 7 Surprisingly Simple Steps. Even then, you likely still have questions. Here are some of the most frequently asked questions I encounter:

Q. Where do these steps come from? Are they your ideas originally?

    A. I have been very intentional about crediting material that I didn't create. Many of these principles and tools originated from some of the great thought leaders over the past hundred years including Dr. Thurman Fleet, Mary Morrissey, Christian Simpson, John Maxwell, Wayne Dyer, Stephen Covey, Napoleon Hill, Viktor Frankl, Paul Martinelli, and Bob Proctor.

    How I've assembled the material is unique to me, as is the title phrase of this book, Choice Is Your SuperPower!®, which I've trademarked.

Q. These 7 steps can't be that simple. What's the catch?

A. There is no catch, and they are that simple! The concepts behind the steps are simple and straightforward. What ISN'T simple is the work required to put these steps into consistent practice. That's where the real work begins. That's why I encourage you to get support to help you in this process, be it an accountability partner, mentor, or Coach. The likelihood of your sustained success is much greater when you have a system of structure and support.

Q. After reading this book, I'm both excited and overwhelmed. Are you suggesting that everyone can be successful if they follow these steps?

A. These steps can apply to everyone, yes. Unfortunately, most people will ignore the basic truths in the book and choose instead to find the fault with the principles vs. turning the inspection inward. Nothing will change in anyone's life if there isn't a deep desire to change and a commitment to doing the hard work of the work. If you are looking for an overnight solution, this is not the book for you. That said, you can begin applying these steps immediately, and will see progress with consistent application.

Q. I've tried visualization before, and it doesn't work for me. I'm good at picturing what I'd love to have in my life, yet nothing changes. And the Jim Carrey story is a one-off and is misleading.

A. If you are consistently visualizing what you'd love to create in your life, that is a great starting point. But it's only the beginning. As you read in Step #6, action is REQUIRED! Without action, all you have are pictures in your head that will never manifest to reality. It's like visualizing the physical shape you'd like to be in but sitting on the couch eating potato chips while you wait for it to happen. It never will. It's the very same thing with visualization. Start with the brain pictures to wire your dream, then create and execute targeted actions to fire the dream. The two together are what ignites the start of your creation.

As far as the Jim Carrey story, I encourage you to do your research as there are literally thousands of stories like Carrey's. You can watch him tell his own story here on YouTube: **Jim Carrey on How He Used Visualisation to Reach His Goals!**

Q. I love the idea of working with you as my Coach, but I can't afford it.

A. I'll be very up front on this. Working with me for 6- or 12- months is a significant investment and is not a partnership for everyone. Not everyone is willing to invest in themselves or their future, or to commit to the hard work described throughout this book. I don't work with everyone as my schedule and time is limited, but I can assure you that, should you decide to explore working with me, and we determine we would be a good fit, you will likely find no greater return on your investment than in working with a Coach. I guarantee that these principles work when you engage them consistently.

So, my question to you is this: Can you afford NOT to change your life? If you're in the same place five years from now, or at the end of your life, is yours a life well-lived to its fullest? If you knew that you could have made a significant investment in creating a life you loved and chose not to do it, I would bet the level of regret you feel will be soul-killing. Even if you don't work with me or another qualified Coach, committing to applying these 7 Surprisingly Simple Steps will enhance your life. It's my hope that you make that commitment to yourself.

"If you want to change the fruit, you will first have to change the root. If you want to change the visible, you will first have to change the invisible." ~ T. Harv Eker

ACKNOWLEDGMENTS

I have been the fortunate recipient of more love, support, teaching, mentoring, and coaching than one person has a right to receive in a single lifetime, from people too numerous to name here. However, there are a few that were so fundamentally instrumental in my growth journey that they must be mentioned and appreciated here, as without their impact, this book would not have been written.

First, to my parents, Dan and Darlene Betzer- there are no adequate words to convey the profound impact you have had and continue to have on my life. From your unconditional love and support to the incredible role models you have been, both spiritually and as life mates, I am eternally grateful. I consider it one of my greatest honors to call myself your daughter.

To my husband, Patrick Dredden, your presence in my life is the gift that keeps on giving. I count every day with you as joy. It bears repeating- you are my best choice.

To my Coach, Christian Simpson- without you, I wouldn't be a Coach, or a successful Business Owner or published Author. Your influence on my life is immeasurable. Thank you for holding me to the highest standards in this industry. You make me better.

To some of the most significant thought leaders, mentors, and influencers who contributed to my lifelong journey of continual personal growth and the evolution of my thinking, I want to thank:

- Mary Morrissey
- Paul Martinelli
- John Maxwell
- Stephen Covey
- Napoleon Hill
- Dr. Thurman Fleet
- Wallace Wattles
- James Allen
- Wayne Dyer
- Bob Proctor
- Maxwell Maltz

Lastly, and most importantly, I humbly thank our Creator, with whom all things are possible.

ABOUT THE AUTHOR

Deb Dredden is a leading Mindset Expert and Executive Coach and is the Founder of Deb Dredden Transformational Coaching, LLC.

In addition to running her own company, Deb is a Founding Member of the Conscious Coaching Academy, the world's only Elite Influencer Coaching Accreditation™ - independently assessed and verified by the industry's longest and most established Accreditation body, the European Coaching & Mentoring Council.

Deb has over 30 years of professional Coaching experience, both in her 2+ decades as an Executive and Officer in the retail field, and now with her own Coaching business. She has worked with Fortune 50 - 500 companies, such as Walmart, LBrands, Samsonite, and more, and in that time has helped thousands of people achieve their personal and professional goals.

Deb is happily married to the love of her life, Patrick Dredden, and they reside in Salt Lake City, Utah, with their two cats, Cali and Dallas. She is an avid reader, loves photography, hiking, and traveling, and is a person of deep faith and consciousness.

You can read more about Deb at her website: **Deb Dredden Transformational Coaching**, as well as on her social media accounts under the same business name on Linkedin, Facebook and Twitter.

Facebook: https://www.facebook.com/DDTC19
LinkedIn: https://www.linkedin.com/company/deb-dredden-transformational-coaching/
Instagram: https://www.instagram.com/ddtc18
Twitter: @Deb Dredden
Email: deb@debdredden.com
Website: debdredden.com

APPENDIX/RESOURCES

Tools/Resources that appeared throughout this book:

Circle of Life Balance Exercise: Complimentary

Which Circle Am I In? Exercise: Complimentary

5-Step Blueprint to Find Your Passion and Begin Living Your Life With Purpose

Gratitude Journal: Complimentary PDF

Additional Tools/Resources that support the 7 Surprisingly Simple Steps

WEBINAR: Being Mindful in the Midst of Chaos: Complimentary

5 Steps to Transform Your Pain into a Lifetime of Gain!: Complimentary PDF

13 Ways to Begin Living Your Passion: Complimentary PDF

10 Proven Power Principles for a Successful and Rewarding Life: Audio Download

The Power of Mindset to Change Your Life!: Online Course

Book a Discovery Call with Deb: Link to my Calendar/ Application

NOTE: Courses, Products, and Services prices listed above are as of August 2022 and are subject to change in the future.

Made in the USA
Las Vegas, NV
24 November 2024

12586153R00066